WOMAN OF GOD

CINDY
BUNCH

10 STUDIES
FOR INDIVIDUALS
OR GROUPS

Life
Builder
Study

INTER-VARSITY PRESS
36 Causton Street, London SW1P 4ST, England
Email: ivp@ivpbooks.com
Website: www.ivpbooks.com

Originally published in the United States of America in the LifeGuide® Bible Studies series in 2001 by InterVarsity Press, Downers Grove, Illinois
First published in Great Britain by Scripture Union in 2001
This edition published in Great Britain by Inter-Varsity Press 2020

British Library Cataloguing-in-Publication Data
A catalogue record for this book is available from the British Library.

ISBN: 978–1–78359–863–2

Printed in Great Britain by 4edge Ltd, Hockley, Essex

Inter-Varsity Press publishes Christian books that are true to the Bible and that communicate the gospel, develop discipleship and strengthen the church for its mission in the world.

IVP originated within the Inter-Varsity Fellowship, now the Universities and Colleges Christian Fellowship, a student movement connecting Christian Unions in universities and colleges throughout Great Britain, and a member movement of the International Fellowship of Evangelical Students. Website: www.uccf.org.uk. That historic association is maintained, and all senior IVP staff and committee members subscribe to the UCCF Basis of Faith.

Contents

Getting the Most
Out of *Woman of God*

At a major Christian conference I attended, a young African American speaker began her talk by saying, "I looked in the mirror this morning, and I thanked God for the beautiful woman he created."

How many of us would—or could—make that kind of statement in public?

My first thought was to write the speaker off as prideful. I thought, *Such an attitude is surely un-Christian.* But the more I pondered it, the more I appreciated the positive self-image she exuded. This was a person who was clearly ready to be used by God. I realized it was my attitude that needed checking.

Most women struggle with issues of self-esteem. Why? To put it simply, we live in a fallen world. One of the great sins of our culture is that we try to put people into boxes. We say such things as "Women aren't good analytical thinkers" and "Men just aren't sensitive." These labels make us feel inferior when we can't, or don't want to, live up to them. Worse yet, they limit our opportunities to use our talents.

In these studies we will explore what it means that God has created us as women who are uniquely gifted. Studies one, four, seven and ten frame the guide with biblical characters who offer us inspiration and creative examples of how to be responsive to God's call in life's hard places. The other studies fill in character qualities that we need to serve God. We will see how Christ's great love can empower us in the midst of our sin-filled world. And most of all, we will begin to understand who God wants us to be.

Have you really looked in the mirror lately? When you do, thank God for creating such an extraordinary human being. A woman.

Suggestions for Individual Study

1. As you begin each study, pray that God will speak to you through his Word.

2. Read the introduction to the study and respond to the personal reflection question or exercise. This is designed to help you focus on God and on the theme of the study.

3. Each study deals with a particular passage—so that you can delve into the author's meaning in that context. Read and reread the passage to be studied. If you are studying a book, it will be helpful to read through the entire book prior to the first study. The questions are written using the language of the New International Version, so you may wish to use that version of the Bible. The New Revised Standard Version is also recommended.

4. This is an inductive Bible study, designed to help you discover for yourself what Scripture is saying. The study includes three types of questions. *Observation* questions ask about the basic facts: who, what, when, where and how. *Interpretation* questions delve into the meaning of the passage. *Application* questions help you discover the implications of the text for growing in Christ. These three keys unlock the treasures of Scripture.

Write your answers to the questions in the spaces provided or in a personal journal. Writing can bring clarity and deeper understanding of yourself and of God's Word.

5. It might be good to have a Bible dictionary handy. Use it to look up any unfamiliar words, names or places.

6. Use the prayer suggestion to guide you in thanking God for what you have learned and to pray about the applications that have come to mind.

7. You may want to go on to the suggestion under "Now or Later," or you may want to use that idea for your next study.

Suggestions for Members of a Group Study

1. Come to the study prepared. Follow the suggestions for individual study mentioned above. You will find that careful preparation will greatly enrich your time spent in group discussion.

2. Be willing to participate in the discussion. The leader of your group will not be lecturing. Instead, he or she will be encouraging the members of the group to discuss what they have learned. The leader will be asking the questions that are found in this guide.

3. Stick to the topic being discussed. Your answers should be based on the verses which are the focus of the discussion and not on outside authorities such as commentaries or speakers. These studies focus on a particular passage of Scripture. Only rarely should you refer to other portions of the Bible. This allows for everyone to participate in in-depth study on equal ground.

4. Be sensitive to the other members of the group. Listen attentively when they describe what they have learned. You may be surprised by their insights! Each question assumes a variety of answers. Many questions do not have "right" answers, particularly questions that aim at meaning or application. Instead the questions push us to explore the passage more thoroughly.

When possible, link what you say to the comments of others. Also, be affirming whenever you can. This will encourage some of the more hesitant members of the group to participate.

5. Be careful not to dominate the discussion. We are sometimes so eager to express our thoughts that we leave too little opportunity for others to respond. By all means participate! But allow others to also.

6. Expect God to teach you through the passage being discussed and through the other members of the group. Pray that you will have an enjoyable and profitable time together, but also that as a result of the study you will find ways that you can take action individually and/or as a group.

7. Remember that anything said in the group is considered confidential and should not be discussed outside the group unless specific permission is given to do so.

8. If you are the group leader, you will find additional suggestions at the back of the guide.

1

Ready for God's Call

Mary's Quiet Trust

Luke 1:26-38, 46-55

I don't often hear God's voice. But I vividly recall one occasion when I was wrestling with what I felt God was calling me to. I said, "I can't do that." (Dumb thing to say to God!) He said, "I am all you need." Simple. Isn't that like God? Yet we spend our whole lives trying to get this truth right.

GROUP DISCUSSION. How do you respond to the notion of hearing God's call? Is it something you have experienced, or is the idea of hearing God a little unreal?

PERSONAL REFLECTION. What would you like for God to talk to you about?

What do you fear hearing from God?

In this study we tackle a familiar passage about a thirteen-year-old girl. Try to read it with fresh eyes, and experience the wonder of Mary's choice to praise God. *Read Luke 1:26-38, 46-55.*

1. What did Mary think and feel as the angel spoke to her (vv. 26-38)?

2. How is Mary's attitude reflected in verses 29, 34 and 38?

What do verses 46-55 reveal about Mary's character?

3. Knowing what God was asking Mary to do, how do you feel reading this passage?

4. What facts do we learn about Jesus from verses 31-35?

5. Why is Mary given the information about Elizabeth (v. 36)?

6. How do you respond to hearing "nothing is impossible with God" (v. 37)?

7. What does Mary mean when she calls herself "the Lord's servant"?

8. Focus on verses 45-55. What strong words and phrases express Mary's feelings about God?

9. God is calling Mary to a very difficult task. Instead of worrying or complaining, she recognizes that he is honoring her (vv. 48-49). What experience have you had of being called to an honorable, but difficult, task? Give an example if you can.

10. What other kinds of good things does Mary praise God for in verses 50-55?

11. How can remembering what God has done in the lives of others help us to be faithful to God's call?

12. In what way would you like to be more like Mary in your response to God?

Offer prayers of gratitude and praise for what God has done in your life and in the lives of those around you already. Offer him yourself. Ask him to make you ready to respond to his call.

Now or Later

13. Reread verse 28. What would it be like to have God call you "highly favored"?

14. How do you think God feels about you? Explore this question in prayer.

2

Content

Overcoming the "If Only" Syndrome

Philippians 4:10-20

"If I only had . . ."

How would you fill in the blank? Would it be "a little more money"? "a day off"? "someone to date"? "a new car"? Sometimes we think that contentment is just around the corner. If we could only have this one elusive thing, our lives would be complete.

But it never happens.

GROUP DISCUSSION. What "one thing" do you sometimes find yourself thinking would bring you contentment?

PERSONAL REFLECTION. Off the top of your head, name three things you're grateful for.

Reflect on your response. (How long did it take you to think of things you're grateful for? Did they come to mind quickly or slowly? How conscious are you of God's good gifts?) What did you learn about yourself?

In his letter to the Philippians Paul writes of a much richer contentment than we can find in the world around us. *Read Philippians 4:10-20.*

1. From this passage, how would you describe the tone of the letter?

2. When in your life might you have written a letter like this?

3. What has the Philippian church done for Paul?

4. In verses 11 and 17-18 Paul emphasizes that he isn't asking for further gifts. Why do you think this is?

5. What does Paul mean when he says that he has learned "the secret of being content" (vv. 11-13)?

6. How is the strength of Christ an encouragement to you when you feel discontented?

How is the support of other Christians an encouragement to you when you are discontented?

7. What do you learn about Paul from verses 15-16?

8. How has verse 19 been real for you?

9. This passage's description of how we find contentment stands in sharp contrast to the messages we receive from the media about finding contentment. How do these contradictory messages make it difficult to trust that God will meet all your needs?

10. What do you need to learn from Paul's example here?

Ask God to show you the sources of godly contentment all around you.

Now or Later

Do not let a day go by this week without thanking God for one gift each day brings. Even if it is difficult for you to really feel thankful at first, persist in prayer. Eventually the feelings will follow your actions.

3

Wise

The Eyes of Faith

Ephesians 1:3-23

The wisdom of women is passed down generation to generation to shape our minds and hearts. Here are some bits of wisdom:

"Real success is willingness to accept God's place for us today."—Ann Kiemel, author

"God don't always come when you think he should, but he's always on time."—Alex Haley, quoting his grandmother

"The ghosts of things that never happened are worse than the ghosts of things that did."—L. M. Montgomery, in *Emily's Quest*

"To be a close follower of Jesus was to learn not to ask, 'Exactly what will it be like?' but to ask rather, 'What must I do to be ready for it?' "—Monica Hellwig, theologian

GROUP DISCUSSION. Which of the above sayings do you find especially wise from your own beliefs and experience? Explain.

What favorite quotes from women would you add to this list?

PERSONAL REFLECTION. Think about some of the women who are looked to as wise in our culture. Who do you think is wise? Why?

While some of the women who are held up as models for us have only worldly wisdom, our world *is* filled with signs of the wisdom of godly women. This study will be an opportunity to celebrate that fact—and to reflect on how we gain biblical wisdom. *Read Ephesians 1:3-14.*

1. List everything verses 4-5 tell you about how God created us.

2. What has God given us in Jesus Christ (vv. 6-10)?

3. What has God given us in the Holy Spirit (vv. 13-14)?

4. Why has God given us so much (v. 12)?

5. *Read Ephesians 1:15-23.* What gifts is Paul asking God to grant the Ephesians?

Why do we need each of these gifts?

6. Why do you think Paul prayed specifically for "the Spirit of wisdom and revelation"?

7. What does it mean to have "the eyes of your heart enlightened" (v. 18)?

8. How do you feel knowing that God's power (described in verses 19-23) is available to you?

9. In what area(s) of life do you feel you might have a unique ability to offer wisdom?

---

10. What do you think being a woman adds to your perspective on wisdom?

Pray that God would enlighten "the eyes of your heart" so that "you may know the hope to which he has called you" (Ephesians 1:18).

Now or Later

Make a commitment to do something that will help you to grow in wisdom and knowledge about Christ. It could be reading a particular book, joining a Sunday school class, praying regularly with someone, or learning more about meditating on Scripture, fasting or anything else you feel a spiritual hunger to learn about.

4

Strong

Deborah in Battle

Judges 4:1—5:9

"On her shoulder, Mary Slessor carried her adopted baby. Clinging to her skirt was her five year old, and with her right hand she coaxed along her three year old. Two older children sloshed behind. Sloshed, because they were trudging through a mangrove swamp in West Africa. It was night. . . . They could not see any snakes that might lie across the path or drape from trees above. But they could hear leopards. To keep the big cats at bay, Mary belted out hymns. The children chimed in.

"Because no missionary had the time, or perhaps, the courage to go, Mary Slessor and her children were moving in to live with the fierce Oyokong people in what is now Nigeria. The year was 1888."*

GROUP DISCUSSION. Name some ways you have seen women show great courage.

Sometimes the courage of women is overlooked because it is expressed differently from the ways men show courage. How have you found this to be true or untrue?

PERSONAL REFLECTION. Who is the most courageous woman you know and why?

The context for this study is that the Israelites were repeatedly selling themselves out to idol worship. God would then turn them over to an evil king. This cycle had already taken place several times. *Read Judges 4.*

---

1. How do these verses describe Israel?

How does Deborah's character contrast with Israel's (vv. 4-7)?

---

2. How does Barak's response exemplify the attitude of Israel (vv. 8-9)?

---

3. How does Deborah show her faith and courage in verses 14-16?

4. What does Barak's response to her instruction further reveal about Deborah's character?

5. How does Jael show courage and initiative in verses 17-22?

6. Do Jael's situation and action feel similar to or different from your life today? Why?

7. Looking back through chapter 4, what are the results of Deborah's act of courage?

8. Chapter 5 is Deborah's poetic retelling of the battle. *Read Judges 5:1-9.* What does she say about God in these verses?

9. What have Deborah and Barak learned about following God?

10. How has stepping out in faith taught you about God?

11. In what areas of your life would you like to act with courage?

Pray for courage in the areas that have come to mind.

Now or Later

This week find a creative way to affirm a woman you know who has demonstrated great courage.

---

*Miriam Adeney, *A Time for Risking* (Portland, Ore.: Multnomah Press, 1987), pp. 147-48.

5

Trustworthy

Standing in the World

Luke 16:1-15

Savvy. Hip. Aware. Technologically literate. These are the qualities of the players who lead our society. *Trustworthy?* The word sounds almost quaint to our ears.

GROUP DISCUSSION. What does it mean to be trustworthy? What are the qualities of a trustworthy person?

PERSONAL REFLECTION. What experiences have you had with putting your trust in someone who is not trustworthy?

What does that feel like?

In Christ's parable being trustworthy is more than just avoiding negative behaviors like stealing, lying and cheating. Being trustworthy involves active behaviors. We must make the most of what we are given, using the unique abilities we have been given. *Read Luke 16:1-15.*

---

1. What key words highlight the main topics in this passage?

---

2. What thoughts or feelings would you have had if you were one of the disciples hearing this story?

---

3. Why was the manager going to be fired (vv. 1-2)?

---

4. Describe the action the manager took (vv. 3-7).

---

5. What benefit did the manager expect to receive from his actions (vv. 3-4)?

---

6. Why did the master commend the manager (vv. 8-9)?

7. From this passage explain the difference between being "dishonest" and being "shrewd."

8. What are the principles Jesus is highlighting in verses 10-13?

9. How does Jesus' teaching in verses 9-13 relate to the story he told?

10. In what ways do the values of the world (v. 5) make it difficult to be a trustworthy woman?

11. How could you make better use of what has been entrusted to you?

Ask God to mold you into a person whom he can call trustworthy.

Now or Later

Begin to analyze your own motives at work and in relationships with others. Are you being a shrewd manager of the resources you have been given? Or are you being dishonest with yourself and others for the sake of your own interests?

6

Forgiving

Beginning with Yourself

There's a lot of pressure on women to "be good." A look at a classroom of five-year-olds quickly shows up differences in the ways boys and girls are socialized. Little girls learn to seek affirmation for following the rules, while boys learn to get attention by breaking the rules. The result in adult women, especially Christians, can be a judgmental attitude. When someone hurts us, we easily slip into bitterness. Forgiveness is difficult for those of us who spend our lives "being good."

GROUP DISCUSSION. What expectations and attitudes do you think contribute to feelings of moral superiority?

PERSONAL REFLECTION. As you begin this study, search your heart: Who do you need to work toward forgiving?

Jesus' teaching on the Sermon on the Mount covers many topics regarding our inner attitudes and outer actions. *Read Matthew 7:1-2* to set the context for the study.

---

1. How do you feel when you read these verses?

---

2. What do you think Jesus means when he says that we will be judged as we judge others?

---

3. *Read Psalm 51.* From the language and tone of this psalm, how would you describe David's feelings about himself at the time he wrote this?

In what ways do you identify with those feelings?

---

4. What is revealed about David's relationship with God in these verses?

5. Focus on the phrase in verse 3, "my sin is always before me." How would this attitude help prevent judgmentalism?

---

6. How do the qualities described in verse 6 help in counteracting sin?

---

7. What kinds of changes does David want to see within himself (vv. 7-12)?

Which of these would you like to see within yourself?

---

8. What does David expect will be the result of his choice to turn from sin (vv. 13-15)?

How have you seen this to be true in your life or in the lives of others?

9. What different meanings does the word *sacrifice* have in verses 16-19?

What does this reveal about what God wants from us?

10. How would cultivating the attitudes described here help you to be a forgiving (not judging) person?

Pray, confessing your sin and asking to be a person who offers grace to others who sin.

Now or Later

If a person you need to forgive, or situation in which you need to practice forgiveness, has come to mind, make that a topic of prayer and action this week.

If a sin of your own toward another person or toward God has surfaced, confess it in prayer and perhaps to a trusted friend.

7

Resourceful

Abigail's Creative Rescue

1 Samuel 25:1-42

Quilters is a musical that depicts the life of early settlers in the American West from a female perspective. An elderly mother makes her daughters a quilt in which each block represents an aspect of her life. She tells desperate stories of piecing scraps late into the cold nights to ensure that her family had adequate warm covering. She describes community gatherings to make quilts for others who were in need. Finally, she describes beautiful festive quilts made in honor of the times of celebration in her life. Quilts are just one example of the resourcefulness and creativity our foremothers modeled for us.

GROUP DISCUSSION. Give an example of how a woman you know is resourceful.

PERSONAL REFLECTION. What are some ways that women are likely to be resourceful which might be overlooked by the larger society?

In this study we will meet a godly woman who used her own ingenuity to save her family. *Read 1 Samuel 25:1-42.*

---

1. What words and phrases throughout the passage describe Nabal?

What would it be like to be married to a man like this?

---

2. Why did David feel justified in asking Nabal for gifts (vv. 7-8, 15-16, 21)?

---

3. What does Nabal's response reveal about him (vv. 10-11)?

---

4. What do you learn about Nabal's household from the way the servant approaches Abigail in verses 14-17?

---

5. What competing needs and concerns does Abigail face at this point?

In what ways do you identify with her situation?

---

6. Describe Abigail's actions in verses 18-31.

---

7. What do Abigail's words and actions reveal about her?

How is this an example of the resourcefulness of women?

8. How does David respond to her (vv. 32-35)?

---

9. In what areas has God granted you resources with which you can serve others?

How can you better use your resources?

Pray for the wisdom to discern how to use your resources and resourcefulness to serve God.

Now or Later

Whether it is a commitment on a large or small scale, find a way to put into action the abilities you thought of in response to question 9.

8

Beautiful

The Fabric of Holiness

1 Peter 3:1-7

What are some of the messages we have received about beauty? We may feel that we should look like the women in the *Sports Illustrated* swimsuit issue or Victoria's Secret models. Or perhaps you recall your mother saying something like "Beauty is as beauty does." How does God define the beauty of a woman?

GROUP DISCUSSION. What are some ways the world defines *beauty*?

How can the desire to measure up to worldly definitions of beauty be used to control or manipulate?

PERSONAL REFLECTION. When do you feel beautiful (or at least pretty good about yourself)?

The following passage reveals God's perspective on inner and outer beauty. *Read 1 Peter 3:1-7.*

---

1. What are the characteristics of a holy woman according to this passage?

---

2. What emotional response do you have as you read this passage?

---

3. What does it mean to be "submissive" as described here (vv. 1-2, 5-6)?

How would this make a person beautiful?

---

4. How do verses 3-4 define *beauty?*

5. Do these verses imply that we should not wear makeup or jewelry, perm our hair, spend money on nice clothing and so on? Explain your response.

---

6. How do you balance the amount of time and energy you put into body versus spirit?

What helps you to balance your physical and spiritual needs with the other demands in your life? (Do you find that time devoted to friends, family and work make it difficult to tend to your own needs?)

---

7. In what ways is Sarah a role model we should emulate? Draw both from verses 5-6 and from your knowledge of Sarah in the Old Testament.

8. Verse 7 describes a husband's response. How does this response flow from the wife's godliness?

---

9. In what ways is the description of beauty in this passage compatible with the world's definition of beauty?

incompatible?

---

10. When have you been surprised and pleased to see the world recognize a godly woman?

---

11. In what way(s) does your definition of beauty need to change?

12. In what way(s) does your attitude toward your own beauty need to change?

Pray that the beauty of the Lord will flourish within you as a testimony of his work to everyone you meet.

Now or Later

Try the following exercise, on your own or with others, to begin looking at how you regard the body God has given you. Name one gift you have in each of these areas. The following lists will help you get started:

Physical	Emotional	Mental	Spiritual
feet	listening	remembering	praying
hands	stability	analyzing	encouraging
figure	patience	comparing	healing
face	empathizing	contrasting	teaching
mouth	supporting	calculating	meditating
hair	understanding	interpreting	giving

How did you feel about doing this exercise? embarrassed? pleased? encouraged? Was it easy or difficult for you?

9

Confident

Evidence of Faith

Hebrews 10:19-25, 32-36

Women write autobiographies very differently from men. Even when they have been very successful, they apologize for their weaknesses and try to explain them, rather than focusing on the positives.*

This is a telling fact. And it is one of many clues suggesting that women often sin not by being overconfident but by being *under*confident. We may think that we are being humble and righteous. In reality we are unwilling or unable to trust ourselves. In the process we reveal our lack of trust in God as well.

GROUP DISCUSSION. What movie or television character exemplifies confidence for you? Why?

PERSONAL REFLECTION. When is it easy for you to express confidence in yourself?

When is it hard?

Read Hebrews 10:19-25.

1. How do these verses tell us that we can be close to God?

2. Why would the original readers of this letter have experienced this as a great privilege (vv. 19-21)?

3. What, according to verse 22, is required to draw near to God?

4. Describe a person you know who holds "unswervingly" to faith.

5. What do verses 24-25 say about how the body of Christ gives us confidence?

How has the body of Christ given you confidence personally?

6. *Read Hebrews 10:32-36.* What situation is described in verses 32-34?

How did they encourage each other to maintain faith?

7. How does a woman's self-confidence relate to her ability to maintain confidence in God?

---

8. When are you tempted to "throw away your confidence"?

---

9. What enables you to maintain confidence in Christ?

Thank God for "his incomparably great power for us who believe" (Ephesians 1:19).

Now or Later

Consider what your own level of confidence is. To what extent do you allow that lack of confidence to keep you from serving God? Confess your difficulties to God. Ask him to give you strength and faith so that you can use the gifts you have been given to their fullest.

---

*Carolyn Heilbrun, *Writing a Woman's Life* (New York: W. W. Norton, 1988), p. 22, quoted in Mary Ellen Ashcroft, *Temptations Women Face* (Downers Grove, Ill.: InterVarsity Press, 1991), p. 29.

10

Ready for God's Grace

Ruth & Naomi's Redemption

Ruth 1 & 4

Have you ever studied the Proverbs 31 woman? She seems to have it all—businesswoman, mother, woman of God. It can be overwhelming to try to live up to the example she sets. It can be overwhelming to study all the character traits described in this guide! God knows that. And the reality is that no matter how godly we are, life can (and will) fall apart in various ways. At those points the quality of our character is tested. But more important, we are reminded that no matter what we do, only God can redeem.

GROUP DISCUSSION. When do you find that life seems most unjust for yourself or for others?

PERSONAL REFLECTION. When have you felt bitter toward God? Why?

We turn to the book of Ruth for a picture of two women who found themselves alone and without resources. As you read this account, keep in mind that Moab was a pagan country and Bethlehem a Jewish country. *Read Ruth 1.*

1. Look closely at the geographical information given here. What would have been difficult about Ruth's situation?

2. What does Naomi seem to be like from this passage?

3. In what ways do you identify with her reaction to her situation at this point (vv. 11-13, 19-21)?

4. What does Ruth's speech in verses 16-18 reveal about her?

5. What do you admire about Ruth from what you have seen of her so far?

---

6. Ruth and Naomi's situation is a reminder that no matter how fine our character is or what our relationship with God is, sometimes life can fall apart. How do you feel when faced with this reality?

---

7. *Read Ruth 4.* In chapter 3 Ruth asked Boaz to serve as kinsman-redeemer by marrying her. In chapter 4 we see Boaz giving a closer relative the opportunity first, as was culturally appropriate. Describe the exchange between Boaz and the other relative.

8. Look at 4:13-17. How has God redeemed what was lost in Naomi's and Ruth's lives?

9. How is the term *kinsman-redeemer* an apt one for what we see happen here?

10. This is a story both of how wrong life can go and of how God can redeem it beyond our wildest expectations. In what ways can this story be an encouragement to you?

Offer praise to our God, who always promises to redeem.

Now or Later

Reflect on the powerful word *redeem*. What would you like God to redeem in your life? Talk to him about it.

Leader's Notes

Leading a Bible discussion can be an enjoyable and rewarding experience. But it can also be *scary*—especially if you've never done it before. If this is your feeling, you're in good company. When God asked Moses to lead the Israelites out of Egypt, he replied, "O Lord, please send someone else to do it!" (Ex 4:13). It was the same with Solomon, Jeremiah and Timothy, but God helped these people in spite of their weaknesses, and he will help you as well.

You don't need to be an expert on the Bible or a trained teacher to lead a Bible discussion. The idea behind these inductive studies is that the leader guides group members to discover for themselves what the Bible has to say. This method of learning will allow group members to remember much more of what is said than a lecture would.

These studies are designed to be led easily. As a matter of fact, the flow of questions through the passage from observation to interpretation to application is so natural that you may feel that the studies lead themselves. This study guide is also flexible. You can use it with a variety of groups—student, professional, neighborhood or church groups. Each study takes forty-five to sixty minutes in a group setting.

There are some important facts to know about group dynamics and encouraging discussion. The suggestions listed below should enable you to effectively and enjoyably fulfill your role as leader.

Preparing for the Study

1. Ask God to help you understand and apply the passage in your own life. Unless this happens, you will not be prepared to lead others. Pray too for the various members of the group. Ask God to open your hearts to the message of his Word and motivate you to action.

2. Read the introduction to the entire guide to get an overview of the entire book and the issues which will be explored.

3. As you begin each study, read and reread the assigned Bible passage to familiarize yourself with it.

4. This study guide is based on the New International Version of the Bible. It will help you and the group if you use this translation as the basis for your study and discussion.

5. Carefully work through each question in the study. Spend time in meditation and reflection as you consider how to respond.

6. Write your thoughts and responses in the space provided in the study guide. This will help you to express your understanding of the passage clearly.

7. It might help to have a Bible dictionary handy. Use it to look up any unfamiliar words, names or places. (For additional help on how to study a passage, see chapter five of *How to Lead a LifeBuilder Study*, IVP, 2018.)

8. Consider how you can apply the Scripture to your life. Remember that the group will follow your lead in responding to the studies. They will not go any deeper than you do.

9. Once you have finished your own study of the passage, familiarize yourself with the leader's notes for the study you are leading. These are designed to help you in several ways. First, they tell you the purpose the study guide author had in mind when writing the study. Take time to think through how the study questions work together to accomplish that purpose. Second, the notes provide you with additional background information or suggestions on group dynamics for various questions. This information can be useful when people have difficulty understanding or answering a question. Third, the leader's notes can alert you to potential problems you may encounter during the study.

10. If you wish to remind yourself of anything mentioned in the leader's notes, make a note to yourself below that question in the study.

Leading the Study

1. Begin the study on time. Open with prayer, asking God to help the group to understand and apply the passage.

2. Be sure that everyone in your group has a study guide. Encourage the group to prepare beforehand for each discussion by reading the introduction to the guide and by working through the questions in the study.

3. At the beginning of your first time together, explain that these studies are meant to be discussions, not lectures. Encourage the members of the group to participate. However, do not put pressure on those who may be hesitant to speak during the first few sessions. You may want to suggest the following guidelines to your group.

☐ Stick to the topic being discussed.

☐ Your responses should be based on the verses which are the focus of the discussion and not on outside authorities such as commentaries or speakers.

☐ These studies focus on a particular passage of Scripture. Only rarely should you refer to other portions of the Bible. This allows for everyone to participate in in-depth study on equal ground.

☐ Anything said in the group is considered confidential and will not be discussed outside the group unless specific permission is given to do so.

☐ We will listen attentively to each other and provide time for each person present to talk.

☐ We will pray for each other.

4. Have a group member read the introduction at the beginning of the discussion.

5. Every session begins with a group discussion question. The question or activity is meant to be used before the passage is read. The question introduces the theme of the study and encourages group members to begin to open up. Encourage as many members as possible to participate, and be ready to get the discussion going with your own response.

This section is designed to reveal where our thoughts or feelings need to be transformed by Scripture. That is why it is especially important not to read the passage before the discussion question is asked. The passage will tend to color the honest reactions people would otherwise give because they are, of course, supposed to think the way the Bible does.

You may want to supplement the group discussion question with an icebreaker to help people to get comfortable. See the community section of the *Small Group Starter Kit* (IVP, 1995) for more ideas.

You also might want to use the personal reflection question with your group. Either allow a time of silence for people to respond individually or discuss it together.

6. Have a group member (or members if the passage is long) read aloud the passage to be studied. Then give people several minutes to read the passage again silently so that they can take it all in.

7. Question 1 will generally be an overview question designed to briefly survey the passage. Encourage the group to look at the whole passage, but try to avoid getting sidetracked by questions or issues that will be addressed later in the study.

8. As you ask the questions, keep in mind that they are designed to be used just as they are written. You may simply read them aloud. Or you may prefer to express them in your own words.

There may be times when it is appropriate to deviate from the study guide. For example, a question may have already been answered. If so, move on to the next question. Or someone may raise an important question not covered in the guide. Take time to discuss it, but try to keep the group from going off on tangents.

9. Avoid answering your own questions. If necessary, repeat or rephrase them until they are clearly understood. Or point out something you read in the leader's notes to clarify the context or meaning. An eager group quickly becomes passive and silent if they think the leader will do most of the talking.

10. Don't be afraid of silence. People may need time to think about the question before formulating their answers.

11. Don't be content with just one answer. Ask, "What do the rest of you think?" or "Anything else?" until several people have given answers to the question.

12. Acknowledge all contributions. Try to be affirming whenever possible. Never reject an answer. If it is clearly off-base, ask, "Which verse led you to that conclusion?" or again, "What do the rest of you think?"

13. Don't expect every answer to be addressed to you, even though this will probably happen at first. As group members become more at ease, they will begin to truly interact with each other. This is one sign of healthy discussion.

14. Don't be afraid of controversy. It can be very stimulating. If you don't resolve an issue completely, don't be frustrated. Move on and keep it in mind for later. A subsequent study may solve the problem.

15. Periodically summarize what the group has said about the passage. This helps to draw together the various ideas mentioned and gives continuity to the study. But don't preach.

16. At the end of the Bible discussion you may want to allow group members a time of quiet to work on an idea under "Now or Later." Then discuss what you experienced. Or you may want to encourage group members to work on these ideas between meetings. Give an opportunity during the session for people to talk about what they are learning.

17. Conclude your time together with conversational prayer, adapting the prayer suggestion at the end of the study to your group. Ask for God's help in following through on the commitments you've made.

18. End on time.

Many more suggestions and helps are found in *How to Lead a LifeBuilder Study*.

Components of Small Groups

A healthy small group should do more than study the Bible. There are four components to consider as you structure your time together.

Nurture. Small groups help us to grow in our knowledge and love of God. Bible study is the key to making this happen and is the foundation of your small group.

Community. Small groups are a great place to develop deep friendships with other Christians. Allow time for informal interaction before and after each study. Plan activities and games that will help you get to know each other. Spend time having fun together—going on a picnic or cooking dinner together.

Worship and prayer. Your study will be enhanced by spending time praising God together in prayer or song. Pray for each other's needs—

and keep track of how God is answering prayer in your group. Ask God to help you to apply what you are learning in your study.

Outreach. Reaching out to others can be a practical way of applying what you are learning, and it will keep your group from becoming self-focused. Host a series of evangelistic discussions for your friends or neighbors. Clean up the yard of an elderly friend. Serve at a soup kitchen together, or spend a day working in the community.

Many more suggestions and helps in each of these areas are found in the *Small Group Starter Kit.* You will also find information on building a small group. Reading through the starter kit will be worth your time.

Study 1. Ready for God's Call. Luke 1:26-38, 46-55.

Purpose: To learn from Mary's quick obedience to God's call.

General note. "In Judaism 'virgins' were young maidens, usually fourteen or younger. The term Luke uses here for 'virgin' also indicates that she had not yet had sexual relations with a man" (Craig Keener, *The Bible Background Commentary: New Testament* [Downers Grove, Ill.: InterVarsity Press, 1993], p. 190).

Question 1. Find some information in the passage: "greatly troubled," "wondered" (v. 29), "do not be afraid" (v. 30). Then use your imagination to picture what it would have been like for Mary to hear these words. Steve Hayner summarizes some of what Mary would have experienced: "fear (who wouldn't quake at the appearance of Gabriel in your back yard?), confusion (sex education had never prepared her for this!), the pangs of rejection (families and fiancés have a hard time understanding this sort of thing), and no doubt some loneliness" ("Notes from the Journey," InterVarsity Christian Fellowship, December 1999).

Question 5. Craig Keener puts it this way: "The point of 1:36-37 is that God, who acted for Elizabeth as he did for Sarah, could still do anything" (*Bible Background,* p. 190). Sarah's story is in Genesis 18:9-15.

You might find it interesting to compare Zechariah's response in the section just preceding this (Lk 1:11-25) to Mary's response.

Question 6. Encourage honest responses to this key verse. Some may be in a place in life where this is hard to believe or accept. Some may feel that God has deserted them or let them down. Others may be at a place of strong faith and have stories to share of God's redemption.

Question 7. Encourage group members to describe in their own words what it means to be God's servant.

Steve Hayner writes of Mary: "It wasn't that she never questioned God's intentions of God's plans. But somehow Mary knew that her life was not finally her own. 'In life and in death,' says a great confession of the Church, 'we belong to God.' Mary believed this truth and it released her from the bondage of all else. She could let go of the worry, the frustration, the fear, the worldly ambition, the jealousy of other peoples' lives, the apparent failures, and even the control which she, like so many of us, probably craved" ("Notes").

Question 8. If you feel that your group would be comfortable, pause here and allow several minutes of quiet individual prayer and meditation so that these powerful words can seep in before you discuss them.

Question 9. This question might seem odd because we can see that it is an honor to bear the Son of God. In question 4 we explored the wonderful truth God was revealing about who Jesus is. Yet when God is calling us to honorable tasks in our own lives, the difficulty may sometimes mask the honor when we first hear the call.

Study 2. Content. Philippians 4:10-20.

Purpose: To explore what contentment is like and what the source of it is.

Question 1. Notice the words that indicate Paul's joy: in verse 10 "rejoice" and in verses 11 and 12 "content." He expresses confidence in Christ's provision in verses 11-13. He expresses gratefulness for the help he received from the Philippians and goodwill toward them (vv. 14-19).

Question 3. In verse 15 Paul says that at the beginning of his ministry in that area, the Philippians were the only ones giving to him. They continued supporting him even when he left the area (v. 16). They have recently sent gifts (vv. 10, 18).

Question 4. It may be suggested that Paul is actually asking for gifts, in a roundabout way. The tone of the letter, however, seems sincerely grateful. Don't let disagreement over this throw you off track.

Question 5. The focus on Christ's provision in verse 13 should lead you to a response.

Question 7. Paul is not bitter although he was wronged by the church. He focuses on the positive side—the gifts that were given. Skip this question if it was already covered in your discussion of question 3.

Question 8. Discuss concrete ways and actual situations in which you have experienced God meeting your needs.

Study 3. Wise. Ephesians 1:3-23.

Purpose: To explore the depth and power of true wisdom.

Question 1. We were chosen before our creation, have been made holy and blameless, and are made his children through Jesus Christ.

Question 3. Craig Keener says the following about the Holy Spirit:

> A wax seal would have a mark of ownership or identification stamped in it, identifying who was attesting what was inside the container that had been sealed. Because it was commonly understood that the Spirit would be made especially available in the time of the end, Paul here speaks of the Spirit as a "deposit" (NIV)—a term used in ancient business documents to mean a "down payment." Those who had tasted the Spirit had begun to taste the life of the future world that God had promised his people. (*Bible Background,* p. 542)

Question 5. He asks for "the Spirit of wisdom and revelation" (v. 17), that the "eyes" of our hearts would be "enlightened" and that we would know the hope to which he has called us, the "riches of his glorious inheritance" (v. 18), and his great power (v. 19).

Question 7. The literal reference would be to the mind or inner discernment and understanding. Move beyond that to consider the implications of such understanding.

Study 4. Strong. Judges 4:1—5:9.

Purpose: To discover what it means to be a woman of strength who can influence and inspire people to God's glory.

Question 1. Read Judges 3:12-31 for the background of Israel's pattern of disobedience. Ehud was God's deliverer from an evil king. God had given Israel over to the king after they disobeyed. Deborah was a prophet and thus was called to speak words from God, in this case to Barak.

Question 2. Verse 9 tells us that Barak was acting cowardly because he didn't trust God.

Question 3. Deborah trusts in the Lord's command despite Barak's doubt. She reminds Barak that the king heads up the army (see, for example, 1 Sam 8:20). This spurs him into action.

Question 4. It is clear that she possesses the strength of God and speaks with the authority of God. For Barak the advantage of having a prophet along would be the feeling that God's presence in the battle would be more real, and both troops and leaders would be more optimistic.

Question 5. Jael seems to be working on her own. She has devised a way to get Sisera into the tent. She carries out her plan quickly and effectively.

Question 6. This is an opportunity for group members to explore more of their own response to this story. It may seem surprising and disturbingly violent to many. There's no right answer to this question.

Question 7. Note what happens in the lives of Deborah, Barak, Jael and especially the Israelites (vv. 23-24). One person acting in faithfulness can have a rippling effect on the faith of those around them.

Question 8. Remembering a victory in song was a traditional practice (see, for example, Ex 15:1-18). Verses 4-5 refer to the Lord's appearance in a storm cloud to lead Israel into Canaan (see Ex 13:21).

Study 5. Trustworthy. Luke 16:1-15.

Purpose: To consider what it means to be a woman in whom others can put their trust.

Question 1. Note the words *master* (v. 3), *dishonest* (v. 8), *shrewd* (v. 8), *worldly* (v. 9), *wealth* (v. 9), *trustworthy* (v. 11) and *servant* (v. 13).

Question 3. Apparently the manager was being wasteful and neglectful of his master's business (v. 1). In verse 8 he is also called "dishonest."

Question 4. The master may have been overcharging the debtors because the Mosaic law didn't allow him to charge interest. Thus the manager may have simply returned the debts to their original amounts and satisfied both the master and the debtors. Or the manager may have been cheating his master by not collecting what was owed to him. Either way, the manager was wisely planning his own future (Kenneth Barker, ed., *The NIV Study Bible* [Grand Rapids, Mich.: Zondervan, 1985], p. 1571).

Question 5. Knowing that he was going to be out of work, the manager planned for the future by lowering the debts of those who owed his master money. This caused the debtors to be obligated to him.

Question 7. In this passage Jesus equates shrewdness with careful planning and skillful deal making. Dishonesty is equated with wastefulness and neglect (v. 1).

Question 8. The literal reference would be to the mind or inner discernment and understanding. Move beyond that to consider the implications of such understanding.

Question 9. In verse 9 Jesus points out that the one way for the steward to ensure that he has a heavenly home is to begin using resources well in daily life. "Worldly wealth" refers not only to money but to all the things of this world. "Although these things—your property, ability, time—belong to this life only, says Jesus, yet what will happen to you then, when you pass into that [eternal] life, will depend on what you are doing with them here and now. Make sure that your use of them brings you into a fellowship of friends which will survive beyond death" (Michael Wilcock, *The Message of Luke* [Downers Grove, Ill.: InterVarsity Press, 1979], p. 160).

Study 6. Forgiving. Matthew 7:1-2; Psalm 51.

Purpose: To understand what it means to forgive others as God has forgiven us and to be aware of our own sin.

General note. The background for Psalm 51 is 2 Samuel 11—12. David committed adultery with Bathsheba and then had her husband murdered to try to cover it. In chapter 12 Nathan confronts David, and he begins to understand what he has done before God.

Question 2. Craig Keener says that "those who seek to judge others now will answer then for usurping God's position" (see also 6:12-15). We tend to apply teachings to others rather than ourselves. However, Jesus points out that "we are objects of God's evaluation, and God evaluates most graciously the meek, who recognize God alone as judge." At the same time Keener reminds us that Jesus is not suggesting that we should not "discern truth from error (see 7:15-23)" or offer appropriate correction (*Matthew,* IVP New Testament Commentary [Downers Grove, Ill.: InterVarsity Press, 1997], pp. 156-57).

Question 3. Take time with reading these verses as they are very powerful and loaded with evocative language. You might have someone prepared ahead of time to read it all through. Also, allow people time to read back through it silently. Then offer a prayer before you begin discussing it. Be aware that this is a powerful and convicting psalm and just putting it in front of people may have a deep impact.

Note the strong repeated plea for God's grace in verse 1: "mercy," "unfailing love," "great compassion." And the plea for renewal in verses 1 and 2: "blot out," "wash away," "cleanse me."

Question 5. Draw out important truths here. Awareness of our own sin helps us to forgive others.

Question 6. *The NIV Study Bible* points out that verse 6 highlights the "great contrast" between David's actions and what God has been teaching him. He moves from here to a "renewed prayer for pardon" in verses 7-9 (Barker, *NIV Study Bible,* p. 831).

Question 8. There is an interesting shift here from David's inner life to his outward witness. He is saying that he will witness to others of the change that God has worked in him. Truly turning from sin brings a powerful testimony: you have probably seen this to be true in the lives of people you know.

Study 7. Resourceful. 1 Samuel 25:1-42.

Purpose: To consider how a woman's ingenuity can help and protect those around her.

Question 1. Nabal was a "Calebite," a descendant of Caleb. According to *The NIV Study Bible,* "since Caleb's name can mean 'dog,' Nabal is subtly depicted as a dog as well as a fool" (Barker, p. 412). Verse 3 tells us he was "surly and mean." His servants describe him as a "wicked" man whom no one can talk to (v. 17). Abigail also calls him "wicked" and "fool" (v. 25).

Question 2. David is asking for a reward for his protection of Nabal's men when they were in his territory. According to the Word Biblical Commentary, "His ten-person delegation . . . carried out a detailed and respectful protocol. David addressed Nabal as 'my brother' . . . wishing peace to the man himself, to his whole household, and to everything he had. The narrator wants us to understand that David sought neither to harm Nabal and his family nor to diminish him in any way of his lavish holdings. . . . David's self-designation as son displayed reverence and respect" (Ralph W. Klein, *1 Samuel*, Word Biblical Commentary [Waco, Tex.: Word, 1983], p. 248).

Question 4. In a patriarchal culture it seems unusual that the servant would have approached Abigail after the master of the house had already given instructions. Further, he seems to expect that she might take some action to rectify the situation. The respect she has earned in her household already is a further testament to Abigail's wisdom and resourcefulness.

Question 5. To our eyes it may appear that Abigail is covering for her good-for-nothing husband. But a "household" in this context was a large unit that included shepherds and other workers. She is protecting a large group of people—and her own well-being. At the same time she risks Nabal's wrath, and we have already been told that he is "wicked" (v. 17). It is also risky for her to go and meet David alone; she is probably taking her life into her hands.

Question 6. Note especially that Abigail worked quickly (v. 18); she personally rode to meet David (v. 20); she showed humility before David (v. 23); she accepted the blame for what had happened (v. 24); she asked for God's blessings on David (vv. 26, 28-31).

Question 7. When Abigail spoke with David, her words were carefully chosen and persuasive. This action kept David from the shame of fighting a fool (Klein, *1 Samuel*, p. 249), from shedding blood and from overstepping his bounds to gain victory. These latter two would have been a discredit to his royal character. "Whereas David boldly refused the opportunity to kill Saul in chapters 24 and 26, only the

action of Abigail prevents him from blood guilt in the case of Nabal"
(ibid., p. 251).

Question 9. Consider natural and spiritual gifts as well as physical
and material resources.

Study 8. Beautiful. 1 Peter 3:1-7.

Purpose: To discover what true beauty is like and how we can develop
it.

General note. Be aware that this topic and passage may be difficult
for some in the group. Many of us struggle with self-consciousness
and feelings of inferiority regarding our own beauty.

Question 1. A holy woman is described as "submissive" and able to
win over an unbeliever by her words and actions (v. 1). She has
"purity" and "reverence" (v. 2). She is not showy or ostentatious (v.
3). Her beauty comes from the inside, reflecting a "gentle and quiet
spirit" (v. 4).

Question 2. There are numerous aspects of this passage that people
might have a strong reaction to. Many have been burned by teachings
on submission, which we will explore further in question 3. Others
may react to the high standard of purity and inner beauty here, perhaps even feeling that such expectations are fake. Some may feel
judged by the suggestions in verse 3, which we will explore later in
their cultural context. Some may find the simplicity of this text free-
ing. It's a lot more straightforward than the detailed monthly beauty
secrets we find in magazines like *Cosmopolitan.*

Question 3. "Submissive" here does not imply a lower status or inferiority. Rather, the passage as a whole seems to suggest a gracious attitude that is concerned with the needs of others. Some may interpret
this as a reference to the principle of "headship" as alluded to in Ephesians 5:22-33. Others may focus on Ephesians 5:21, which commands
all believers to submit to one another "out of reverence for Christ."
The point here is not to get into an in-depth discussion about views of
headship and marital authority but to discover how a humble and
submissive spirit enhances our beauty.

Question 7. For background on Sarah see Genesis 12:10-20 and 18:1-
15.

Question 8. See also Ephesians 5:25-33 for the husband's responsibilities.

Now or Later. If your group is close, you might try doing this together. Or allow time for people to work through it on their own and then discuss it as a group. You could even pair off and fill out the chart for each other as a way of affirming one another.

Study 9. Confident. Hebrews 10:19-25, 32-36.

Purpose: To find confidence in God and in ourselves through faith.

Question 1. This passage tells us we can be close to God through Jesus' blood (vv. 19-20) and by drawing near to God in faith (v. 22).

Question 2. Verse 20 refers to the curtain in the temple which separated the Holy Place from the Most Holy Place—where only the priests were allowed (Ex 26:31-33). When Christ died, it was ripped in two (Mk 15:38), signifying that all people were now able to enter God's presence.

Verse 21 refers to Jesus as a priest. He intervenes with God on our behalf as a priest would according to Old Testament law. As noted above, in the temple the priests had certain privileges such as entering the holy of holies to be in God's presence. Through Christ's blood we are all given equal opportunity to approach God and communicate with him.

Question 3. Four factors are required to approach God: (1) a sincere heart, (2) full assurance of faith, (3) freedom from a guilty conscience and (4) bodies washed with pure water. This last requirement does not refer to an "external ceremony such as baptism but [is] a figure for inner cleansing, of which the washing of the priests under the old covenant was a symbol (see Ex 30:19-21; Lev 8:6 . . .)" (*NIV Study Bible,* p. 1871). However, depending on denominational perspectives, group members may differ on the *NIV Study Bible* interpretation of verse 22. Some may see it not as a symbol but as a reminder of the sacramental nature of baptism in offering real internal cleansing. Either way, the reference to water points us to the need for inner cleansing.

Question 5. Verses 24-25 tell us to encourage each other on to love and good works. Take time to consider what this means. Then move into what it looks like on a practical level. For example, when have you been challenged by other believers to try something new like leading a small group or teaching children's Sunday school and found it rewarding?

Question 7. If we don't see ourselves as powerful, it may be because we don't believe that we are deeply loved by a God of power and strength. Further, if we don't believe that we are uniquely gifted, it may be that we doubt or discount God's call to us. If we are crippled by sin, unable to confess it to the Lord and hear his forgiveness, then our ministry will be diminished. Conversely, as we grow in our confidence in God, we will grow in our ability to act in faith knowing that we are filled with the very Spirit of the Lord we worship.

Study 10. Ready for God's Grace. Ruth 1 & 4.
Purpose: To be reminded that it is God who redeems our lives and not our own good qualities or actions.

General note. The book of Ruth is quite brief, and you may want to read through chapters 2 and 3 before the study so that you can fill in any gaps.

Question 1. Ruth is leaving behind everything she knows to stick with Naomi—her land, culture, friends, even her religion.

Question 2. When we read the book of Ruth as a whole, it seems that Naomi was a very fine person. In this chapter we see that her daughters-in-law are very committed to her, most likely a testimony to Naomi. In chapters 2 and 3 she gives Ruth good advice about Boaz. And in chapter 4 we find that she is part of the lineage of David—and Jesus. (But you might not want to discuss this aspect until you get to chapter 4.) At the same time Naomi appears to be very bitter and angry with God about her current situation. Sticking with someone who is expressing feelings like this could be tough.

Question 8. Naomi gains a family again with Boaz and Ruth. And she gains a grandchild. Even greater, this child becomes part of the lineage of David—and of Jesus—as do Ruth and Naomi. Who could have imagined that God would do such wonderful things?

Cindy Bunch is associate publisher and director of editorial at InterVarsity Press. She is also the author and coauthor of several LifeBuilder Bible Studies, including Christian Virtues *and* God's Word.